Edge Hill University
Learning Services

Edge Hill University
LEARNING SERVICES

23/·12/08

The Little Books of Life Skills

In our rapidly changing world, education is becoming less and less about imparting knowledge than it is about empowerment. We now want to make sure our children get the skills they need, not only to engage with and take responsibility for their own learning, but to successfully take part in a range of experiences throughout their lives.

The strategies and activities in the *Little Books of Life Skills* will help children see themselves as champions of their own world, a critical step in meeting the outcomes of the **Every Child Matters** agenda. Each title in the series will help children get the skills they need to enjoy and achieve – in school and beyond.

The five *Little Books of Life Skills* are:

- *Helping your pupils to ask questions*
- *Helping your pupils to be resilient*
- *Helping your pupils to communicate effectively and manage conflict*
- *Helping your pupils to think for themselves*
- *Helping your pupils to work cooperatively*

Helping your pupils to communicate effectively and manage conflict

Lynette Longaretti and Robyn English

Routledge
Taylor & Francis Group

LONDON AND NEW YORK

First published by Curriculum Corporation 2005
PO Box 177
Carlton South Vic 3053
Australia

This edition published 2008 by Routledge
2 Park Square, Milton Park, Abingdon, Oxon, OX14 4RN, United Kingdom

Simultaneously published in the USA and Canada
by Routledge
270 Madison Ave, New York, NY 10016

Routledge is an imprint of the Taylor & Francis Group, an informa business

© 2008 Lynette Longaretti and Robyn English

Typeset in Stone Serif by FiSH Books, Enfield, Middx.
Printed and bound in Great Britain by TJ International Ltd, Padstow, Cornwall

Dedication
To Ella Ariane: the precious things in life. (LL)
To three great teachers and friends: Sue D, Sue B and Sue Y. (RE)

British Library Cataloguing in Publication Data
A catalogue record for this book is available from the British Library

Library of Congress Cataloging in Publication Data
A catalog record has been requested for this book

ISBN 10: 1-415-44729-1
ISBN 13: 978-1-415-44729-4

Contents

What is the relationship between effective communication and conflict management?

Good communication and interpersonal relationships are essential for effective teaching and learning. They are the basis for many of the issues and concerns that teachers and pupils meet daily. Social and personal behaviours are fundamental elements that cross subject areas and impact significantly on pupil learning success. The different personalities, group dynamics and roles that exist within a school give rise to varying types of relationships and interactions. These communications and relationships are not always constructive or satisfying. In schools, there will always be differences, interpersonal conflicts and disagreements. It is important to keep communications positive but sometimes our inability to communicate effectively can, in itself, create conflict. The way in which teachers manage this conflict is pivotal in determining the ethos of the classroom.

Effective communication

Teachers are faced with endless questions relating to both communication and relationships. Any teacher, regardless of their teaching area or level, will often wonder how to:

- develop rapport with pupils
- communicate with pupils who have little or no English
- handle pupil aggression and conflict
- form partnerships with pupils' parents so that learning and wellbeing is enhanced
- plan, negotiate or disagree about curriculum decisions with their colleagues without causing friction.

This book looks at the characteristics of effective communication and considers the skills essential for forming and sustaining productive relationships. These are fundamental in enhancing a culture of fairness, respect, inclusivity and cooperation in the classroom. Once this culture of positive interaction is established, conflict can be managed with a great deal more success.

Being aware of oneself and expressing oneself is part of communication. The complementary part, important for communication and relationships, is being aware of others – that is, being empathetic. Showing empathy means being able to perceive accurately the experiences of another person. Often we make assumptions about others and their feelings, and we do not check if they are accurate or not. When we are empathetic with others, we check that our assumptions about others are correct. How often do we tell pupils that they should consider others, that they should 'walk a mile in their shoes'? But how often do we take the time to explicitly teach the skills that are necessary to do this?

Teaching is inextricably linked with forming and sustaining ongoing relationships. Effective communication and conflict management skills are therefore essential.

Communication is an area often taken for granted. We tend to assume that being able to speak automatically implies communication, but this is not always the case. It is imperative that teachers and pupils become skilled in the basics of communication to increase an understanding of each other.

The main purpose of being aware of others is to help one person see, feel and understand things from another person's point of view. This requires specific skills, such as the ability to:

- describe behaviour (rather than evaluate it)
- check one's perceptions (ask rather than assume)
- summarise ideas and reflect feelings through active listening
- give and receive feedback non-judgementally and non-defensively.

Communication is a two-way process. For it to flow, teachers and pupils need a repertoire of skills and strategies to use in any given situation. Of course one type of response may not succeed in a different context. The ability to choose the best approach is a skill in itself. This is critical, considering the different pupils, colleagues and parents that teachers interact with every day.

There are several basic ideals in effective communication. These are:

- being genuine – having a true intention to communicate effectively
- being empathetic – understanding that there are other points of view
- being reflective – taking time to consider what is communicated along with what is an appropriate response
- being respectful – having a positive regard for others.

It is useful to regard these ideals as a backdrop against which the key communication skills rest.

Forms of communication

Messages can be sent in a number of forms. They can also be received and understood in different ways. The two main forms of messages presented in this book are verbal and non-verbal communication.

Verbal communication

Teachers need to use verbal communication effectively to ensure personal rights and promote collaboration in the classroom, as well as to head off potential conflict. Verbal communication is what teachers do most of the time. Research has revealed that teachers do most of the talking in classrooms with very little time directed towards challenging pupils to become involved in talking, questioning, problem solving and higher-order thinking.

Non-verbal communication

Non-verbal communication is any form of communication that involves the display of expressions and behaviours or cues (see the table on page 5). Meaning is conveyed not only by what is said and how but also by our actions or by what is not stated. Quite often in the classroom, it is that which has not been verbalised by the teacher that can convey the most powerful messages to pupils.

Non-verbal communication is a powerful form of communication, which we learn unconsciously through socialisation, usually at a very young age. Being able to read non-verbal cues without distorting or over-interpreting them is important; however, the ability to do this is not necessarily innate. We need to teach pupils to recognise non-verbal cues, to learn to use non-verbal communication appropriately and to articulate when negative forms of non-verbal communication are occurring in interactions.

Non-verbal cues include:

- physical movement, such as gestures and distance
- physical characteristics, such as gestures and blushing
- facial expressions, such as smiles, frowns and raised eyebrows
- voice-related behaviour, such as tone, pitch, voice level and pauses.

Speaking skills

Assertiveness is a pertinent verbal skill necessary for good communication and conflict management, but it relies on others having active listening skills.

Active speaking skills

Assertiveness	Application
'I' messages can be used to take initiative and responsibility when communicating. They should clearly express one's opinions, needs, wants, interests and feelings in a non-threatening and non-defensive way without imposing on the rights of others.	Responding assertively means: 1. Describing the behaviour or situation: 'I would prefer not to work on the policy tonight.' 2. Describing your feelings: 'I feel anxious about not meeting the group's request. I feel torn . . .' 3. Describing the consequences for yourself: 'Because I would miss an important appointment.'

Listening skills

Active listening involves a number of components, which can be divided into three broad categories: attending skills, following skills and reflecting skills. See the following table for an explanation of each.

Active listening skills

Label and purpose	Application
Attending skills Appropriate non-verbal skills	Facial expressions, verbal expressions, tone
An appropriate environment	Avoid dealing with issues in a public forum
Physical and psychological orientation to others' personal 'presence'; gives others the message of being 'with them'	Effective eye contact, appropriate distance, body orientation, etc
Puts one in a position to listen to what the other has to say	Minimising distractions (giving full attention to someone); for example, stop what you are doing and face the pupil
Following skills Appropriate cues to help the other begin/continue speaking without interruption	Attending skills, non-advice giving, minimal encouragement (e.g. 'hmmm'), minimal speaking/questioning
Reflecting skills *Clarifying* Request confirmation of what has been said	For example: 'You felt flattered being asked to join the school play?'
Reflective responses Summarise the feeling and factual content of the other's response	For example: 'You are upset because you did not get the part you wanted in the performance.'
Paraphrasing Concise, specific and concrete responses which reflect the other's position	For example: 'So the problem is really about coping with your activities after school. You are unsure whether you can manage those as well as the play.'
Summarising A brief restatement/synthesis of the other's statement	For example: 'You want to find out more about what is involved. How can you do this?'

Conflict resolution

Conflict can be defined as any interaction in which the participants have different goals and perceive that the other person is inhibiting their ability to achieve this goal. It is important to handle conflicts appropriately as they can provide opportunities for learning.

There are a variety of ways in which people attempt to resolve disputes. These can vary from avoidance, negotiation, problem solving, conceding and contending to mediation, arbitration or litigation. Resolving an issue satisfactorily requires the management of emotions and a re-orientation of the management of conflict to return the focus to the actual issue. This is quite a difficult aspect of resolving conflict but it is not impossible. The manner in which we deal with conflict can be viewed in terms of the match between the importance of maintaining a relationship as opposed to the importance of achieving the desired goal or outcome.

HIGH IMPORTANCE

RELATIONSHIPS

Smoothing

Confrontation

Compromise

Withdrawal

Forcing

GOAL ACHIEVEMENT

LOW IMPORTANCE ⟶ HIGH IMPORTANCE

(Adapted from Johnson & Johnson, 1987)

To achieve constructive resolution, the skills of attending, listening, asserting and problem solving are crucial. Techniques and strategies designed to resolve conflict are useful as they can help redefine the problem and assist in finding mutually satisfying solutions to the problem.

The steps to problem solving are:

1. Define the problem
2. Respect and understand other's perspective
3. Assert views and feelings
4. Brainstorm solutions
5. Select a solution and take action.

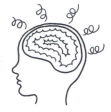

To resolve conflicts both parties must have their needs met. Collaborative problem solving is most effective when there is a shared awareness of needs. Clarifying and staying focused on the issue is important to achieving resolution and meeting both parties' needs. Of course, resolution is not always possible and at these times a mutual third party may be the best solution (that is, mediation). While pupils may often request that the teacher step in and resolve the conflict, teachers should view their role as one of 'manager' in which the pupils are supported and taught to resolve the conflict themselves.

One key role of the teacher is to help pupils consider different ways of dealing with problems and finding alternative solutions. Many pupils find it difficult to predict the possible consequences of actions. Taking time to consider alternatives and to predict the possible outcomes of different actions can be very helpful. A simple strategy is to use an effects wheel like the one on page 9 (see page 46 for a proforma). The group brainstorms a number of possible consequences and then considers the flow-on effect of these.

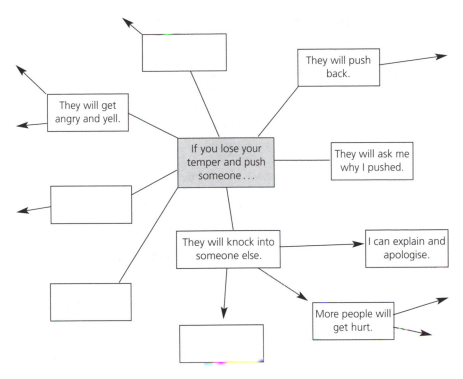

Types of conflict

Conflict occurs across a broad spectrum of situations; for example, it can comprise interpersonal and intergroup conflict in diverse settings. Interpersonal conflict (usually between two or more individuals) is the type of conflict most familiar to teachers. In a school setting this may be between pupils, colleagues, parents or administration. Intergroup conflict describes conflict within the school involving two or more groups of people.

Physical continuum

A physical continuum is an effective strategy to help pupils consider that there is a range of alternative views in a conflict situation – that things are not necessarily black or white. A continuum is an infinite set of points in a line.

Pupils consider their response to a statement in terms of where they would place themselves on a line, requiring them to consider the reasons behind their point of view. They should be prepared to justify their position to others. The example below shows how pupils consider their views on a conflict issue, place themselves on the line and explain the reasons for their position.

Consider your personal position on the line from 'strongly disagree' to 'strongly agree' for the following statements.

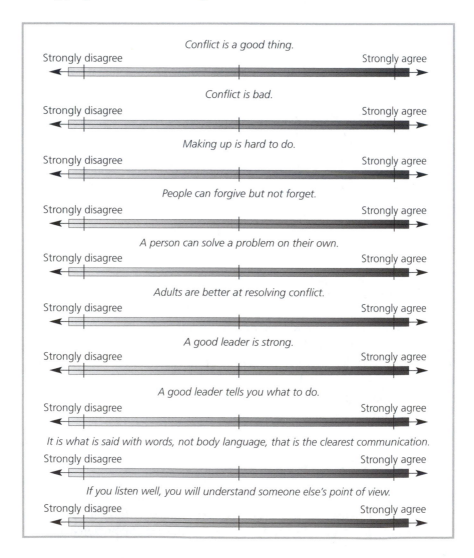

What are the benefits of effective communication and conflict management?

Socialisation is a major component of school life from the very first day of the very first year. It is a context in which self-expression and interpersonal skills are regularly practised and learnt, a time where friendships are formed and established.

Individuals are better able to manage if they have the capacity to deal effectively with others. Opportunities for learning to express emotions, communicate and relate with others appropriately should naturally occur in the school setting. Interpersonal skills are necessary basic skills required in school and society alike.

Sometimes, as educators and adults, we assume that pupils automatically know how to manage stress and solve problems or conflicts that occur at school and at home. Pupils do not necessarily have those skills. We cannot make assumptions about their previous experiences; nor can we assume that once some lessons on 'getting along' have been conducted in the early years of schooling, the skills have been mastered. These skills require regular revision and a strong focus at the beginning of each new school year. By making this a regular focus of the classroom, these skills become explicit and practised.

When pupils are specifically taught strategies for developing effective communication and conflict management, they are better prepared to deal with real-life problems. This acknowledges that pupils need to develop specific self-instruction and management techniques such as:

- assertiveness
- social problem solving
- positive behaviour
- positive thinking

- decision making
- interpersonal skills.

Working together in a cooperative manner allows pupils to become competent in learning skills such as:

- positive interdependence
- face to face interaction
- individual accountability
- interpersonal and small group skills
- reflection
- social skills
- critical and creative thinking skills.

Group work provides a valuable context for developing social skills. The basic skills required for constructive group work are:

- sharing
- taking responsibility
- encouraging others
- active listening
- observing and describing behaviour
- reflection (on group process).

EFFECTIVE GROUPS

- have all their equipment ready
- work together quietly
- work better cooperatively
- use strategies to solve problems
- communicate effectively
- involve all members of the group

These skills are crucial in determining how pupils deal with adversity. Making use of, understanding and learning from the variety of real-life issues and situations that emerge within the classroom and school community leads to productive outcomes for pupils and the whole school.

Scenarios

The school setting is ripe with examples for small groups to use as scenarios for practising problem solving. A group may be given a scenario (see the examples below) and asked to discuss and record appropriate, peaceful and realistic solutions to the problem. Further scenarios are provided on page 47.

One person has told the truth but the second person doesn't believe them.

One person wants to be alone with their friend but another friend wants to join them.

A group of pupils is being harassed by a number of others.

One person wants to play a ball game but their best friend doesn't want to.

Two people have a fight. One of them calls a friend to take their side and support them. The friend thinks the other person is in the right.

The role of the teacher

It is essential that teachers provide pupils with a variety of constructive and cooperative approaches and strategies. It is also crucial to provide pupils with continuing experiences that draw on these strategies in order for them to be rehearsed and developed. Only by making these skills part of every pupil's ongoing repertoire will they learn how to apply social skills, enact positive thoughts and move towards satisfying relationships in their lives. In every classroom, the teacher plays a vital role in developing these skills in pupils, thereby enhancing learning.

Planning for curriculum opportunities

One of the most significant roles of the teacher is to structure a classroom program that allows opportunities for pupils to engage in and practise the skills they need to be effective communicators and conflict managers. These activities need to be:

- planned
- sequenced
- integrated
- varied
- practical
- relevant to the pupils' needs
- interactive
- flexible

Modelling

A widely preferred way of learning a new skill is to watch someone do it well and emulate them. This is very much the case for learning to be an effective communicator, as well as being able to handle difficult situations and disagreements. The way a teacher does this in the school and classroom setting can provide an excellent learning opportunity for pupils. The teacher is an important role model to teach pupils how to appropriately manage and resolve disputes in a variety of ways and to equip them with the necessary skills for a win/win outcome rather than win/lose. By promoting positive behaviour through their interactions with pupils, teachers can encourage them to grow and learn. Helping pupils become more socially adept is easier when teachers' own interactions are positive and promote positive behaviour.

Explicit teaching of social skills

Social skills are learnt behaviours. Pupils come into the classroom with a wide range of behaviours, which can affect how successfully they relate to other pupils and how capable they are at solving problems collaboratively.

In the school context, social skills are defined as those behaviours that a pupil displays toward others. These relate to:

- helping them get what they want
- helping to maintain a good relationship with others
- considering the rights of others
- considering the feelings of others.

In the classroom setting these skills correspond to:

- friendly responsibility
- leadership
- expressing opinions in a positive way
- negotiating
- respecting others' opinions and ideas
- being positive
- being a good winner and loser

- playing fairly
- including others in discussions and decisions
- taking turns and sharing
- suggesting and persuading
- showing tolerance.

(Adapted from McGrath, 1997)

Social skills are interpreted differently across society. Despite this variation, the following behaviours have been identified as important for social competence.

- Eye contact
- Facial expression
- Appropriate distance/personal space
- Quality of voice
- Greeting others
- Making conversation
- Playing/working with others
- Gaining attention and/or asking for help
- Coping with conflict
- Grooming and hygiene

(AusAID, 1999)

In order to communicate effectively and have successful positive relationships with others, pupils need to learn appropriate ways of interacting. It is imperative that teachers understand the need to explicitly teach social skills to all children. What is deemed appropriate may differ between cultures and families, as well as over time. It is important for teachers to acknowledge this but equally important for them to make these variations explicit to pupils. People behave differently in different situations and it can be embarrassing if the 'wrong' behaviour is practised in a particular context. Often, we do not know what the appropriate greeting, behaviour or body language is, when in a new situation. It is helpful for this to be openly stated and explained.

Explicit teaching of effective speaking and listening behaviours

A useful activity to help pupils become aware of the power of non-verbal communication is to set up groups of three to demonstrate communication breakdown. One pupil is the 'listener', one is the 'speaker' and one is the 'observer'. The teacher takes all 'speakers' out of the room and gives them the following instructions:

> Your task is to talk for two minutes to your partner about a topic that you know well and are passionate about. Make them listen to your interesting information.

The teacher then takes all the 'listeners' out and gives them the following instructions.

> The speaker will try to get you interested in what they have to say. You are not interested. Ignore them.

The teacher then takes the observers out and explains the instructions that have been given to the others. The observer's role is to monitor the behaviour of both the speaker and the listener in terms of gaining attention or actively avoiding interactions.

After two minutes of interaction, each person tells the others in their group what they were trying to do. The observers share their observations.

Here are some examples from different groups in one class:

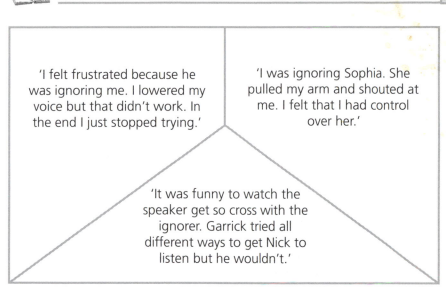

'I felt frustrated because he was ignoring me. I lowered my voice but that didn't work. In the end I just stopped trying.'

'I was ignoring Sophia. She pulled my arm and shouted at me. I felt that I had control over her.'

'It was funny to watch the speaker get so cross with the ignorer. Garrick tried all different ways to get Nick to listen but he wouldn't.'

Mediating conflict

Teachers frequently play a vital role in managing conflict. Although the aim is to support pupils to develop skills so they can resolve conflict independently, the teacher is often needed to support or mediate in a conflict situation. When helping pupils identify and resolve conflicts, remember that resolving differences requires:

- giving pupils your full attention and listening to their feelings
- encouraging and helping pupils to express their feelings in words and listen to the feelings of others
- asking pupils what they have already done to deal with the problem
- summarising the problem as it is understood so far
- acknowledging that the problem exists and the need to sort out a solution together so that pupils are satisfied with the outcome
- providing alternative ways of thinking about the problem
- engaging pupils in the problem-solving process – brainstorming solutions
- reviewing the possible solutions and helping pupils select an appropriate and satisfactory solution

- encouraging pupils to try out the solutions, see if they work for everyone and, if not, try again
- avoiding passing judgement, interrogating, or overreacting or offering advice or opinions too soon.

Personal reflection

Through reflection, we are able to notice and act upon what does and does not work in given situations. This reflection is perhaps the most important aspect of effective teaching. To purposefully watch what is happening in our classrooms and school communities, and to explicitly attempt to address underlying weaknesses and inconsistencies is an important starting place, as well as being essential in monitoring ongoing development.

Reflection is something that most of us don't plan for in our classrooms. Nevertheless, we often find ourselves informally mulling over a lesson or a specific pupil and thinking about what happened and how well we managed the situation. How often do we find ourselves saying, 'If I did that again, next time I'd . . . ', or 'That worked really well, but it would be even better if . . . '? It is these informal reflections that drive our development as teachers. When we do take the time to keep a reflective journal or meet regularly with colleagues to reflect on our practice, we realise how powerful this strategy can be for our own learning.

Organising the classroom

To prepare for a classroom in which communication is going to be effective and conflict managed in a positive and pupil-led manner, three areas need to be considered. The teacher is responsible for making curriculum content decisions, deciding on teaching practices that will be used and preparing a classroom environment and culture that supports pupils and promotes the skills being taught.

Curriculum

Many of the big concepts that form the basis of integrated studies topics have clear links to classroom communication and conflict resolution. Consider how the following concepts can have such a dual application or purpose.

Interdependence	Equity	Identity
Change	Power	Continuity
Resources	Adaptation	Forces
Diversity	Needs and wants	Survival
Safety	Culture	Sustainability

Placing the teaching of effective communication skills within a regular class program, such as an English lesson, gives a valid context to the skill. Integrated topics create an authentic context within which activities that develop personal skills and attitudes can be taught. This allows for communication and interpersonal skills to be introduced, taught and practised within a range of settings. A history topic such as 'Britain at War' naturally lends itself to careful consideration of conflict. Within the world context, individual or school-based conflicts can be raised and strategies taught.

Teaching practices

The actual activities that take place in a classroom are the vehicles through which we teach our content. When planning programs, teachers consider the content carefully and match it to appropriate activities. The skills needed for completing the activities are taught as the activity progresses. The key ideas considered in this book are practical and active. It is therefore appropriate to use highly interactive teaching practices to introduce these to the class. Games, role-play, simulations and discussions are all the kinds of activities through which concepts and skills of communication and conflict management can be taught. These are considered in more depth and with suggestions for specific activities later in this book.

Many activities presented here have been purposefully designed to include cooperative learning and group work for the following reasons:

- To better meet the needs and interests of different individuals.
- To build the collective knowledge of the whole class group.
- To encourage application of the skills taught in various group (small to large) contexts.
- To model cooperation and collaboration in the class context.

The skills of effective communication and conflict management require practice and development. This can be achieved in the safe environment of pair and small group work. Interpersonal and communication skills are social. It is not realistic to deal with them out of the social learning context. Cooperative learning contexts highlight the need for effective communication and conflict management.

Environment and culture

An important step in achieving open communication and managing conflict constructively within the classroom is to establish a cooperative and supportive environment. Team building and trust are necessary as the issues involved are highly personal. It is essential that teachers establish a learning community in which individuals respect the rights of others and feel safe enough to take risks with their learning. Ideally, this is done at the beginning of the school year by establishing clear classroom rules or a code of practice. Teachers need to review this regularly and consider the consequences for inappropriate behaviour, to remind all pupils of the practices that are encouraged and those that won't be tolerated. This is also the time when effective conflict management principles and skills can be incorporated into establishing class routines.

A constructive environment

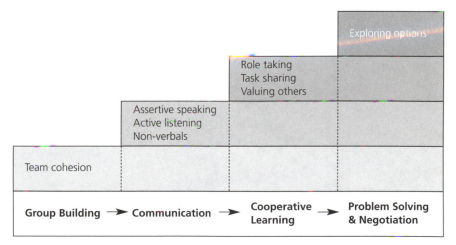

(Allard & Wilson, 1995)

The relationship between pupil and teacher is vital. A positive relationship of mutual trust and respect ensures good communication and a willingness to take appropriate learning risks. Pupils should understand that a good working relationship is not a 'buddy' relationship. Behavioural expectations need to be made clear and explicit, and pupils need to know the boundaries in terms of what can be said and the manner in which it should be communicated. Consistency is essential. Pupils value fairness and are scathing of teachers perceived to have favourites. They can also be quite unnerved by teachers who allow a lax environment one day but are easily angered the next.

Strategies and activities

This section is intended to outline key teaching strategies and provide some sample activities to develop the required skills. Different pupils have different learning styles and, consequently, an activity that is fun and engaging for one pupil might be challenging or threatening for another. It is important to have a wide repertoire of strategies and activities to ensure that as many pupils as possible are catered for over a period of time.

Role-play

Role-play is a valuable teaching and learning strategy that enables pupils to identify and explore emotions, thoughts, behaviours, attitudes and values. Role-play enables pupils to practise new skills and understandings in a safe context. It also enables them to experience and appreciate another's point of view. Importantly, role-play allows pupils to make connections between hypothetical and real-life situations, and make sense of their own and others' behaviour. Complex concepts can be introduced and explored in a supportive and enjoyable context.

Role-play may be used to assist pupils to act out various situations relevant to the social skills being developed. It can be either highly structured or incidental acting out of situations as they arise. Teachers may use role-plays to deal with specific social dilemmas occurring at school, such as bullying, arguments or joining a group game; or to allow pupils to experiment with new experiences or behaviours, such as leading a group, running class meetings or requesting help.

It is important to be sensitive to the fact that although most pupils view role-play as fun, not all pupils like to participate, and that some young children have not yet developed the maturity to distance themselves from the roles they play. Teachers need to lead up to introducing and using the technique in various ways. Similarly, activities need to be debriefed to allow pupils to openly and explicitly explore issues that have arisen. Some suggestions about how to introduce role-play activities are included below.

Roving Mike

The teacher uses a fake microphone to encourage pupils to offer opinions. The teacher makes a statement as if running a TV chat show and asks a pupil at random to express an opinion.

For example:

Teacher: With all this talk of terrorism, the only sensible thing is to cancel all international sporting and cultural events. Mr Q, here, from a major airline is sure to agree. What do you think Mr Q?

Pupil: Well, I think . . .

Footprints

A large pair of cardboard footprints is placed on the floor at the front of the room. A statement is made and a pupil is asked to stand in the footprints to consider and respond from different perspectives.

Propping up with props

Having access to physical props can help pupils take on a different role for a few minutes. A selection of hats, coats and objects such as an umbrella, walking stick or school bag are invaluable aids to the imagination. Putting on a hat or picking up a suitcase can help pupils think of themselves as someone different for a minute.

Some hints when using role-play

- Provide clear directions.
- Ask for volunteers where appropriate.
- Explain the purpose of the role-play session (e.g. it may be skill development).
- Provide space for performing role-play.
- Be comfortable to stop role-play for redirection, feedback, etc.
- Emphasise when pupils are 'in' role and 'out' of role.
- Always take time after the role-play to debrief. This encourages pupils to reflect on their immediate experiences, share insights they may have and share audience responses.

Structured controversy

Controversy is a type of conflict that exists when a pupil's ideas, opinions, conclusions and/or information are incompatible with those of another, and the two seek to reach an agreement (Johnson & Johnson, 1987).

Creating structured controversy is a challenging approach for the teacher, as intellectual conflict is rarely created, managed and resolved within the classroom. This approach can create some anxiety among teachers as classrooms are usually set up for pupils to compromise and quickly agree if difference of opinion arises. Conflict within the classroom is not usually encouraged, yet structured controversy can be a powerful teaching tool.

Structured controversy requires considerable class time to be effective. Reaching consensus on an issue does not happen quickly. It requires at least three class sessions of around one hour. A simple procedure is outlined below.

Steps in structured controversy	Explanation
Group work and pair work	A group of four is created and a topic is presented. Pairs are formed and each pair given one 'side' of the argument.
Investigating an issue and learning the information	Each pair researches the topic from the point of view allocated to them.
Articulating and justifying a position	Each pair states their case to the other pair ensuring that they justify their view fully and explain clearly.
Reversing positions	Pairs take reverse positions and repeat the research and presentation process.
Reaching consensus	Having considered both sides of the case, the team of four works towards a consensus opinion of the topic.

Topics for structured controversy

Junior topics

- Should a bell or music be played at school to signify the end of class?
- Should cartoons or wrestling be on TV for children?
- Should homework be distributed each night or once a week?
- Should you spend or save your pocket money?

Senior topics

- Which is better – ball games or athletics?
- Should Britain remain a monarchy?
- Should pupils use a calculator or do mental maths?

Managing conflict through problem solving

Problem solving is a fun and effective way to explore strategies for resolving conflict. When helping pupils resolve conflict, it is useful to develop some steps that are constructive and pupil-centred. There are many different problem-solving techniques and processes that provide teachers and pupils with a series of steps to follow. Conflict in the classroom may be effectively resolved with a win/win or 'no lose' approach. The value of the five-step problem-solving strategy outlined here (see page 29) lies in the provision of a systematic process of sorting out and clarifying ideas, emotions, needs and conflict. The idea is to use the method consistently and repeatedly so that pupils gradually adopt the method for themselves.

Through problem-solving tasks pupils can learn to develop a variety of solutions to a problem, to consider the outcomes of their actions and to make decisions. However, for effective problem solving it is important that pupils know and understand the procedure, and are skilled in active listening, clarifying the issue and brainstorming. *Cooperative Camping* (page 48) is an example of an activity that can be used with this technique.

Five-step problem-solving strategy

Step	Key purpose	Explanation	Example
1	Define the problem	The starting point of any collaborative problem-solving effort is developing a clear picture of the problem. This means that those in conflict need to be able to state what they think are the issues or problems.	Lin takes Roslyn's special pen from her desk and uses it without asking.
2	Respect and understand others' perspectives	Listening actively until one has experienced the other side can bring about greater understanding. This can be achieved through paraphrasing, that is, reflecting the other person's words and feelings.	Lin listens as Roslyn explains what has happened. Lin paraphrases: 'So you are saying that you did not like me going into your desk?'
3	Assert views and feelings	Being able to express and identify one's point of view, feelings, needs or personal concerns in direct and appropriate ways are essential skills in resolving conflict.	Roslyn expresses her feelings about the situation: 'I was annoyed that you went into my desk without asking. You should have asked!'
4	Brainstorm solutions	Generate solutions so both parties are satisfied with the outcome. Creating options is generally achieved through brainstorming, and requires the ability to brainstorm, recognise needs, cooperate and collaborate.	Together, Roslyn and Lin think of at least three ways to resolve the issue. Lin: 'I can ask your permission next time. I can bring my own pens to school.' Roslyn: 'I can put my pens somewhere that we can both reach. I can leave my special pens at home.'
5	Select a solution and take action	Each person can state their preferred options, and together reach a consensus on one that is appropriate and suitable to both. It is essential that the options selected are appropriate and that agreement is reached about how they will be implemented.	Roslyn: 'I am happy to put my pens out on the desk so we can both reach them, but please don't go into my desk.' Lin: 'I agree with that. Sorry for going into your desk and thanks for sharing.'

(Adapted from Condliffe, 1991)

Simulation

We use the term 'simulation' to describe a model of reality (simplified or complex). We have focused on social simulations to provide a way of exploring people's behaviour. The social simulations we suggest are combined with role-play and game. A simulation game involves a number of players who are required to act out roles according to certain guidelines. The interaction between these role-players is vital to the outcome of the simulation game and crucial to the realism of the simulation.

Simulation games provide a fun context in which pupils can take on a different perspective and explore a problem from a point of view that might not necessarily be their own. Creating simulations with strong, almost stereotypical roles can assist pupils to take another perspective. Some can do this readily, while others find it very difficult to argue a line that is not their own.

The proformas *Hilldale* (page 55) and *Business as Usual* (page 52) have been developed to explore conflict within a curriculum context. *Hilldale* uses an environmental education context while *Business as Usual* uses a local community and commerce base.

Discussion

The purposes and techniques for discussion suggested in this book differ depending on the context, task and questions asked. In all cases, however, discussion:

- provides pupils with an opportunity to share experiences, insights and concerns in a safe context

- encourages pupils to clarify, review and argue their point of view

- requires pupils to listen to other views and perspectives, insights and ideas

- requires pupils to reflect on their own and others' behaviours, verbal and non-verbal language and participation in discussions.

Circle Time

Circle Time (Bessell & Palomares, 1973) is a whole class discussion and sharing time in which no responses or answers are considered to be 'wrong'. The teacher or a pupil provides the beginning of a sentence and a pupil completes it. Over time and with practice, the teacher can take a lesser role in responding to comments as pupils take more responsibility for running the discussion themselves. In this technique:

- all pupils sit in a circle so they can all see each other
- one person speaks at a time
- participants may choose to speak or pass to the next person
- all contributions are acceptable
- there are no wrong answers, as participants are expressing their own views and feelings.

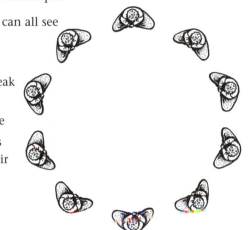

Talk tokens

A strategy that can be useful for encouraging all pupils to participate in class discussions and also in helping pupils learn the process of turn taking in discussions is 'talk tokens'. At the beginning of a discussion session each pupil is given a number of tokens. These can be counters or pieces of card. As they make a contribution to the discussion  they give up a talk token. When there are no tokens left, that person can no longer speak but must continue to listen to others.

This strategy can be used in large or small group discussions. The pupil decides when and how they contribute to the discussion rather than waiting until the teacher selects them to say something. This technique is also very effective for censoring dominating talkers as they have to ration their contribution. Using talk tokens highlights the process of turn taking in discussion and reinforces active listening.

Fishbowl

The fishbowl technique is one in which a small group acts as an 'example' and conducts a discussion seated in the middle of the room with the other class members circled around them as observers. This is a useful strategy as it allows many pupils to take on the role of observer and then share their observations in a debriefing session. It is important that this is not seen as an opportunity to criticise those in the centre, but rather to make non-judgemental comments about what was seen and heard.

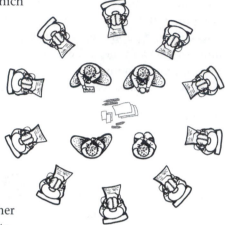

Doughnut discussion

Two equal circles of pupils are created, one inside the other. Each pupil on the inner circle faces a pupil on the outer circle, creating the shape of a doughnut. After a few minutes of discussion with this partner, the teacher gives an instruction to one circle, either the inner or the outer, to move on to the next person in the other circle. Rotation does not have to move one by one. The teacher can add a complication by asking, for example, the inner circle to move three places in a clockwise direction. In this way discussion partners are somewhat random and are frequently changed. This strategy is particularly effective for moving pupils away from only selecting discussion partners from their friendship group.

Reflection

Building a regular reflection time into class lessons can be as powerful for pupils as it is for teachers. There are endless activities and strategies to support pupils in considering the purpose of the lesson, the success they had in developing skills and understandings from it and, importantly, the plans they have to use or adapt this learning in the future.

These strategies can be as simple as posing the questions:

- What skills have I used?
- How effective was my communication with others?
- Have I reached a conclusion or agreement with others?

Questionnaires can add a greater degree of structure to reflection (see *My Conflict Style*, page 56). After pupils have completed the questionnaire, pairs, small groups or the whole class can consider the advantages and disadvantages of having different styles in relation to resolving conflict.

Frequently asked questions (and troubleshooting)

Does the conflict management process really work with pupils?

This model (see page 8) does work but it needs to be taught and practised in order to become second nature. We all slip back into old habits and ways of doing things. If the skills of conflict resolution and management process are not practised, and pupils are not given the appropriate skills and language for this, then they will not become accustomed to applying it to everyday interactions. Teachers should also be modelling these in their everyday interactions.

Is it too late to teach older kids the skills and process of conflict management?

We often think it is too late as pupils are older and it should have been covered in primary school, but not all pupils develop appropriate interpersonal skills as children. If we don't teach the skills for appropriately resolving issues, we are doing pupils a disservice. As teachers, we cannot assume these skills have been taught in the past, nor can we assume that our pupils are proficient in using them because of their age/year level. Secondary school pupils deal daily with complex interpersonal issues – they too need the skills to resolve them, opportunities to practise the skills, and time to reflect and discuss their abilities, responses and associated issues. Secondary school teachers need innovative, relevant and meaningful ways to teach and review the skills, and address the pupils' issues.

How can teachers manage their own emotions in conflicts?

Dealing with conflict when emotions are running hot is not effective. The following tips are helpful in situations where someone is angry or emotional.

- Give yourself an opportunity to release feelings appropriately and away from the situation – take a deep breath, count to 10 (or 100) or walk away. The matter can be delayed and sorted out later with these emotions temporarily put aside (but not ignored/avoided).

- Seek some assistance by talking about the emotions and emotional response with a colleague.

- If the conflict is with a pupil and the teacher is angry or emotional, it is important to leave the situation and return to resolve the conflict when the teacher feels better able to manage their emotions and calmly communicate feelings and thoughts. The teacher must be able to listen to and resolve the issue fairly, and this is not easy to do when emotional.

- Stay focused on the actual situation but allow time to focus on your own feelings. Think and reflect on where these feelings come from and why they occur.

- Express feelings to the other person in conflict without blaming or projecting onto them. This can be seen as an opportunity to improve relations with that person.

- Think of a traffic light:

> **Red** = Stop; time to calm self; use different strategies
> **Amber** = Think/reflect on feelings, triggers, consequences, actions
> **Green** = Go; resolve conflict with a calmer win/win approach

How can you manage a highly emotional situation?

Be in tune with others and actively listen to their feelings. Give the other person some 'space' to express and vent their feelings. Treat them with respect, and communicate respect and tolerance to them from the outset as this is what they will pick up on. Ensure you are talking with them, not at them. Allow them some time to 'let off steam'. Do not retaliate, as this will only escalate the conflict. Keep quiet if necessary so that they feel you have listened and heard what they want to say. State your own feelings and ideas – it helps confirm the emotions involved and directs the conflict management back on to the actual issue.

It is important to keep the discussion focused on the primary issue. Pupils can, when very angry or emotional, respond inappropriately with rudeness or bad language. While this should not be tolerated, the 'heat of the argument' is not the place to pick up on these. They are secondary concerns and should be dealt with separately.

Is there a sequence in which skills for effective communication should be taught?

Speaking and listening skills, both verbal and non-verbal, are interlinked and happen simultaneously when communicating. Pupils demonstrate many of these behaviours naturally in daily interactions with others, but they often lack refinement. It is important, however, that teachers take time in class to explicitly discuss and develop these skills so that they can be used in a more structured and formal way. It is helpful to provide opportunities for pupils to practise strategies so that effective communication becomes part of their natural repertoire.

How often do lessons in communication and conflict management skills need to be undertaken?

There is no given formula for the frequency of lessons. There are a number of considerations, including:

- Taking opportunities to include sessions into the context of integrated studies

- Making sessions ongoing and sequential to ensure development of skills rather than one-off lessons that are easily forgotten
- Ensuring sessions are provided in both informal (e.g. as altercations occur in the yard) and formal (e.g. structured role-plays in the classroom) modes
- Providing ample opportunities to practise and refine new skills.

What do you do if another person is just not listening even though you are being appropriately assertive?

You can't expect to change another person's behaviour, but you do have control over how you respond. If it is clear that the situation is not progressing, despite assertive communication on the part of the speaker, it is better for the speaker to leave the situation to ensure that conflict doesn't escalate.

Tips for the teacher

The following tips summarise key points that underpin effective teaching for conflict management and constructive communication in the classroom.

- While it is useful to have a collection of activities to develop effective communication skills, teachers need to make considered decisions about which activities to use to meet particular needs and address specific issues that may arise.

- It is important for teachers to reflect on their own values and consider how these beliefs and expectations impact on activities.

- A positive and democratic classroom climate is essential. Democracy and dependence, along with independence and interdependence, need to be valued by every member of the class.

- We cannot assume that pupils 'know it' or 'have already done it' when it comes to skills in communication and conflict management. We must explicitly teach and reinforce these skills.

- Every individual needs to feel that they are valued and respected. Pupils will quickly identify whether the messages in the classroom are merely empty rhetoric.

- Thinking and feeling are interrelated processes. It is important to demonstrate to pupils that their thoughts and feelings are connected and can affect each other.

- Teaching and learning should be fun, relevant and meaningful. Planned lessons should involve all pupils in an enjoyable way that is explicitly connected to their own experiences, so that they see the point and acknowledge the relevance.

- Reflection and evaluation are fundamental processes in teaching that inform planning and guide all teaching. Plan for this in lessons to ensure that these processes aren't overlooked.
- Practise assertive 'I' statements in simulated and 'real' contexts.

Assessment and record keeping

The activities in this book are designed to allow pupils to develop skills in effective communication and to be able to manage conflict in a positive and proactive manner. Pupils will therefore need to be assessed in terms of:

■ skill development

■ skill application

■ the ability to reflect on the effectiveness of personal practices.

Assessment, then, will need to take several forms and be conducted in several contexts in order to accommodate pupil difference.

Who assesses?

Pupils need to be able to make judgements about how well they manage different situations. Self-assessment will usually take the form of reflection but this can be supported by structured tasks such as sentence starters and judgement continuums. (See pages 57–64 for sample checklists and continuums.)

Teachers need to make assessment of social skill development a normal and regular part of class evaluation, as with any other skill area. It is important that assessment follows the general guidelines of authentic assessment. It should be:

■ **Ongoing** – It is not appropriate to check for a skill once and assume it has been mastered. By assessing social skill development several times over the year, results will be more reliable and show development rather than simply being either present or absent.

- **Varied** – Pupils demonstrate their understandings in different ways. A range of strategies, activities and presentation forums should be provided to ensure that all pupils have the opportunity to demonstrate their understandings in a number of ways and contexts.
- **Formal and anecdotal** – Formal procedures, such as checklists and activities specifically set up to test pupils' social skills, are one part of the assessment procedure. Equally important is the need for teachers to collect anecdotal evidence of behaviours that demonstrate that pupils have (or lack) certain skills.
- **Provide feedback for pupils** – Pupils are the key stakeholders in their learning in these areas. It is essential that pupils of all ages are given explicit feedback on their abilities to manage effective communication and conflict situations.

How should records of pupil skill achievement be kept?

A number of skill and behaviour checklists are included on pages 57, 58 and 61. These are starting points only – adaptations and variations are encouraged. These checklists serve as records to show development over time. It is important to evaluate pupils' skills in different contexts over a period of time.

While checklists can be helpful, they do not give specific information about the way in which pupils demonstrate skills. Space for comments, extended observations and anecdotal evidence is important. A commonly used strategy is to keep an assessment page for each pupil to collect observational notes as they occur over the school year. (See the example on page 43.)

Speaking skills checklist

Name: Ella S			
Skills	**Date**	**Date**	**Comments**
Makes eye contact with the audience	13/4	16/8	Has a tendency to look down
No put downs	13/4	25/5	Can be sarcastic but witty
Takes turns	13/4	25/5	Is very considerate of including others
Uses appropriate tone	13/4	16/8	At times a bit whiney
Uses appropriate pitch, voice level	13/4	16/8	Appropriate
Uses appropriate pace (pausing, speeding up, slowing down)	13/4	16/8	Satisfactory
Gives ideas	25/5	05/6	Very creative
Talks through a plan	25/5	05/6	Very thorough
Adjusts ideas to suit purpose	25/5	05/6	Uses appropriate concepts
Provides support for ideas	25/5	05/6	Uses persuasive arguments
Verbally encourages ideas	25/5	10/7	Consistently supportive of others in her group
Responds thoughtfully to questions	13/4	10/7	With appropriate consideration
Contributes to group/class discussion	13/4	10/7	Always with careful thought

Proformas for the classroom

9

Effects Wheel

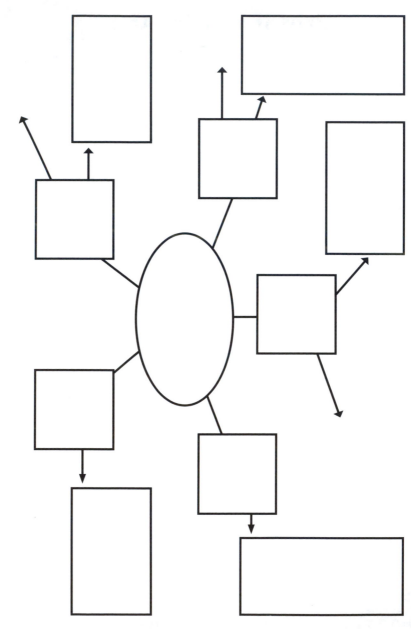

Name: _____

Problem-solving Scenarios

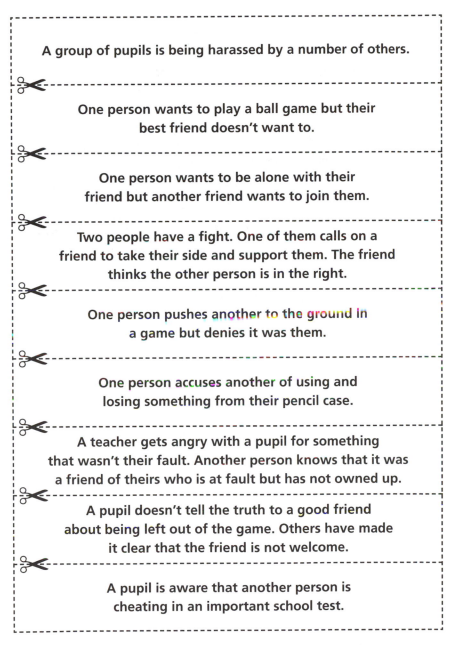

A group of pupils is being harassed by a number of others.

One person wants to play a ball game but their
best friend doesn't want to.

One person wants to be alone with their
friend but another friend wants to join them.

Two people have a fight. One of them calls on a
friend to take their side and support them. The friend
thinks the other person is in the right.

One person pushes another to the ground in
a game but denies it was them.

One person accuses another of using and
losing something from their pencil case.

A teacher gets angry with a pupil for something
that wasn't their fault. Another person knows that it was
a friend of theirs who is at fault but has not owned up.

A pupil doesn't tell the truth to a good friend
about being left out of the game. Others have made
it clear that the friend is not welcome.

A pupil is aware that another person is
cheating in an important school test.

Cooperative Camping

Organise the class into small groups. Provide each group with the list of camping equipment on page 49.

 SET A LIMIT OF 20–30 MINUTES FOR THIS TASK.

Each group selects items from the list to take on a weekend camping trip. The group can only carry six items because they are going into the mountains. They may take seven items if they don't take the tent. Each group must collaborate and reach a consensus about the items they are going to take.

After the allocated time, each group shares their list with the class and explains the reasons behind their choices. As a class, discuss group differences and justifications for each decision. Pupils now return to their groups to see if they want to make changes to the list.

Discuss the process of reaching consensus, the issues faced, the feelings involved, whether or not everyone agreed without argument and how differences were dealt with.

Cooperative Camping Equipment

Imagine your group is going on a weekend camping trip. You will be travelling into the mountains, so you can only carry six items. You can take seven items if you don't take the tent. In your group, decide which items you will take.

- a tent
- a box of matches
- 5 cans of baked beans
- a kerosene lamp
- a torch
- a stove
- a 4 litre container of water
- 4 camp beds
- 2 packets of butter
- a dozen eggs
- 3 loaves of bread
- a book
- 12 metres of rope
- a fishing line
- 1 length of material
- a compass

Simulation Game: Business as Usual

Preparation

- Provide each pupil with the 'scenario' text (page 51). It is beneficial to read it through as a class and discuss the information to ensure everyone understands the situation presented.

- Provide each pair of pupils with a 'decision sheet' (page 52) and ask them to complete the table using dot points to identify pros and cons of each option. Rank the options.

- Form small groups in which different decision sheets can be discussed. The group might be asked to come to a consensus about the most ideal option.

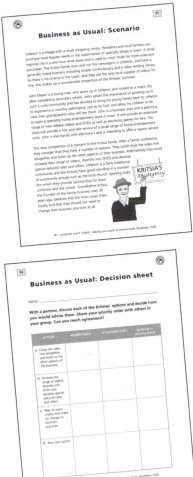

© L. Longaretti and R. English, *Helping your pupils to communicate*, Routledge, 2008.

Business as Usual: Scenario

Littleton is a village with a small shopping centre. Residents and local farmers can purchase most regular needs in the supermarket or specialty shops in town. A small regional city is a one-hour drive away and is used by most locals for more extensive purchases. The Kritsia family own and run the newsagent in Littleton, and have a generally mixed business including simple confectionery and a video lending library. As there is no cinema in the town, and they are the only local supplier of videos for hire, this makes up a considerable proportion of the Kritsias' turnover.

John Meyer is a young man who grew up in Littleton and moved to a major city after completing secondary school. John values the importance of growing up in such a rural community and has decided to bring his young family back to Littleton to experience a 'country upbringing' just as he had, and allow his children to be near their grandparents who still live there. John is a business man and is planning to open a speciality home entertainment store in town. It will provide an extensive range of new release videos and DVDs as well as electronic games for hire. The store will provide a hire and sale service of a small range of home entertainment units. John is also handy with electronics and is intending to offer a repairs service.

This new competition is a concern to the Kritsia family. After a family conference, they consider that they have a number of options. They could close the video hire altogether and build up the other aspects of their business. Alternatively they could increase their range of videos, diversify into DVDs and develop special reduced rates and offers. Littleton is a fairly traditional community and the Kritsias have good standing in a number of community groups such as the local church, sporting clubs (for which they provide sponsorship for team uniforms) and the school. Grandfather Kritsia, the founder of the family business over 30 years ago, believes that the town owes them loyalty and that they should not need to change their business practices at all.

KRITSIA'S newsagency

Business as Usual: Decision sheet

Name: _____

With a partner, discuss each of the Kritsias' options and decide how you would advise them. Share your priority order with others in your group. Can you reach agreement?

OPTION	ADVANTAGES	DISADVANTAGES	Ranking in priority order
a) Close the video hire altogether and build up the other aspects of the business.			
b) Increase the range of videos, diversify into DVDs and develop special reduced rates and offers.			
c) Rely on town loyalty and make no change to business practices.			
d) Your own option.			

Simulation Game: Hilldale

This activity is designed for the whole class. The class is organised into small groups and uses the 'expert jigsaw' strategy (see the procedure below) to prepare for a simulated advisory meeting. The simulation relates to environmental and land use issues.

Context

A parcel of crown land has been handed over to the local council of Hilldale. It is up to the council to determine the land use zone of the land and how it is to be used. A meeting has been called so that several people who represent different interests in the community can put forward their plans and arguments to guide the council's decision.

Land description

The land is an irregular shaped block of five hectares. It is gently undulating and is currently in its natural state of open woodland with several large open clearings. A permanent creek cuts across one corner. The land is adjacent to farmland on its east boundary, residential housing on the south and west boundaries and woods on the north boundary.

Procedure

- Divide the class into groups of six so that all roles are used (see page 55). These are the 'home groups'.
- Explain the scenario to the class by reading the context and land description.
- Explain that each member of the group will take on a different role and, after some preparation, will return to the group for a simulated meeting to advise the local council.
- Give the groups a few minutes to allocate roles. Alternatively these can be allocated by ballot or predetermined by the teacher.
- Split the groups so that new groups are formed with each person having the same role (i.e. all the Farmer McDonalds together, all the Olive Greens together, etc).

- These newly formed 'expert groups' spend some time preparing their case, sharing ideas, justifications, notes, questions, etc. Ensure that everyone in the expert group is well prepared to take back all their ideas to their home group. At this stage the teacher will need to move between groups posing questions, giving suggestions and clarifying concerns.

- The teacher needs to work with the Colin Dunkleys to explain his role as a councillor. He will need to keep the advisory meeting on track, make sure everyone gets to say their piece without ridicule and ensure that the time frame is kept. After all cases have been put, Colin will have the decision-making power.

- Re-form home groups. Allocate a time frame within which the advisory meeting will take place. Colin Dunkley will chair the meeting.

- Hold advisory meetings within home groups.

- The Colin Dunkley characters re-form expert groups to share their evidence and the ideas that were put to them in the advisory meetings. As a group they decide which case they will be recommending to the next local council planning meeting.

- The Colins return to home groups and advise them of his decision.

Procedural flowchart

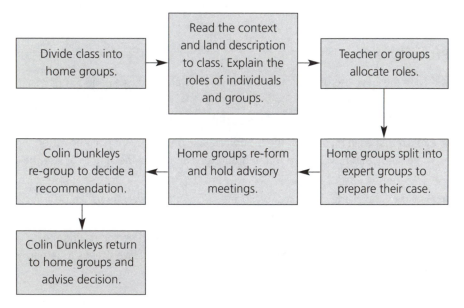

© L. Longaretti and R. English, *Helping your pupils to communicate*, Routledge, 2008.

Hilldale: Character roles

Stakeholders

Farmer McDonald, the owner of the farm that shares a boundary. Up until now her animals have had limited access to the land for extra grazing. She is interested in increasing the size of her land.

✂ -

Jack Jackson, a land developer and building contractor. Jack is interested in using the land for residential development. Housing is in short supply in Hilldale and rental property is scarce.

✂ -

Olive Green, the local representative for the Wildlife Trust, coordinator of local wildlife watch and recycling programs, and science teacher at the secondary school. Olive wants to retain natural habitat and control development of, and access to, the area.

✂ -

Jon Strapp, the president of the local athletics, football and bowls clubs. Jon is keen to expand the sporting facilities available for the growing number of Hilldale residents.

Chairperson

✂ -

Colin Dunkley, local councillor and chairperson of the meeting. Colin is representing the council's building and development committee. His term of office is due to expire in the next six months. He is hoping to be re-elected to the council and is keen to stand for Mayor.

Colin's task is to hear each member's case and to lead discussion between stakeholders. At the end of the meeting Colin will announce his recommendation to council and give the main reasons behind it.

My Conflict Style

Complete this questionnaire. Place a tick under the heading that is most true of you.

When you have a problem with someone, what do you try to do?

	Most times	Sometimes	Never
Avoid the person			
Try to reach an agreement			
Complain or moan until you get your way			
Fight (physically)			
Get another person to decide who is right			
Change the subject			
Give up			
Try to understand the other person's side			
Admit that you are wrong even though you don't think you are			

What do your responses say about your conflict style? Do you generally avoid conflict, become angry or try to reach an agreement?

_____

_____

_____

Verbal Communication Checklist

Name: _____

SKILLS	DATE	DATE	DATE	DATE	DATE	DATE
No put downs						
Takes turns						
Uses appropriate tone						
Uses appropriate pitch, voice level						
Contributes ideas						
Verbally encourages ideas						
Contributes to group/class discussion						
Expresses opinions/points of view in an appropriate manner						
Uses pauses effectively						
Clearly expresses needs/wants						
Clearly expresses feelings, interests						
Asks relevant questions						
Is able to initiate a conversation						
Follows conversation						
Responds assertively in describing behaviour, feelings and consequences (able to use 'I' statements)						

Active Listening Checklist

Name: _____

SKILLS	DATE	DATE	DATE	DATE	DATE	DATE
Attending skills						
Looks involved						
Gets involved						
Uses good eye contact						
Following skills						
Occasionally prompts the speaker (e.g. 'Would you like to talk more about …?')						
Gives some encouragement, such as nodding, some expressions like 'yes' and 'go on'						
Asks limited questions						
Maintains an attentive silence						
Reflecting skills						
Occasional paraphrasing of what the other person has said						
Requests confirmation of what has been said						
Reflects the other person's feelings						
Reflects the other person's meanings						
Summarises what has been said from time to time						

Individual Communication Self-assessment (frequency)

Name: _____ Date: _____

Place an X on the line to show how often you do these things.

I listen to others.

always   mostly   sometimes   not much   never

I show others I am listening by nodding or saying something like 'yes' or 'go on'.

always   mostly   sometimes   not much   never

I look at the person speaking (or use eye contact).

always   mostly   sometimes   not much   never

I listen in silence.

always   mostly   sometimes   not much   never

I encourage others to speak.

always   mostly   sometimes   not much   never

I summarise what the speaker has said.

always   mostly   sometimes   not much   never

I summarise what the speaker means.

always   mostly   sometimes   not much   never

I check my understanding of what I hear.

always   mostly   sometimes   not much   never

Individual Communication Self-assessment (quality)

Name: _____ Date: _____

Place an X on the line to show how you do these things.

I listen to others.

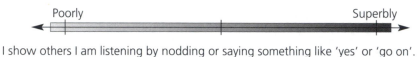

Poorly   Superbly

I show others I am listening by nodding or saying something like 'yes' or 'go on'.

Poorly   Superbly

I look at the person speaking (or use eye contact).

Poorly   Superbly

I listen in silence.

Poorly   Superbly

I encourage others to speak.

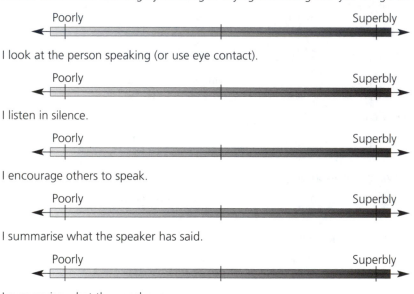

Poorly   Superbly

I summarise what the speaker has said.

Poorly   Superbly

I summarise what the speaker means.

Poorly   Superbly

I check my understanding of what I hear.

Poorly   Superbly

Conflict Resolution Checklist

Name: _____ Date: _____

	Understands	Applies	Reflects
Problem-solving skills			
Brainstorms solutions			
Clarifies ideas			
Confirms ideas by checking own understanding of what was said			
Builds on others' ideas			
Is able to predict possible consequences of solutions			
Is able to constructively criticise ideas (i.e. state points of agreement and disagreement)			
Is able to justify points of agreement/disagreement			
Is able to find solutions			
Managing differences			
Defines the problem			
Willingly works out the problem with others			
Is able to clearly state a position			
Sees the problem from another viewpoint			
Is able to negotiate with another person			
Is able to seek help from others			
Is able to reach an agreement with the other person			
Is able to manage emotions			

Problem Solving Self-assessment

Name: _____ Date: _____

Place an X on the line to show how often you do these things when you have a problem to solve.

I think of a number of different solutions to the problem.

Never   Always

I make my ideas clear.

Never   Always

I check my own understanding of what was said.

Never   Always

I build on others' ideas.

Never   Always

I think of the consequences of the solutions.

Never   Always

I state what I agree or disagree with about another person's ideas.

Never   Always

I give reasons for why I agree or disagree (or for my views).

Never   Always

I am able to find solutions.

Never   Always

Conflict Resolution Self-assessment

Name: _____ Date: _____

Place an X on the line to show how often you do these things when you have a conflict to resolve.

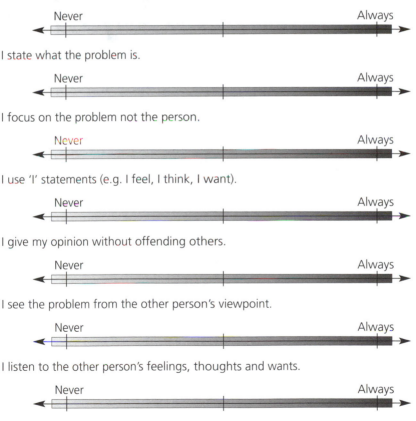

I am willing to work out the problem with others.

Never   Always

I state what the problem is.

Never   Always

I focus on the problem not the person.

Never   Always

I use 'I' statements (e.g. I feel, I think, I want).

Never   Always

I give my opinion without offending others.

Never   Always

I see the problem from the other person's viewpoint.

Never   Always

I listen to the other person's feelings, thoughts and wants.

Never   Always

I negotiate and/or compromise with the other person.

Never   Always

I seek help from others.

Never   Always

I look for solutions that will satisfy everyone in the conflict.

Never   Always

I am able to reach an agreement with the other person.

Never   Always

I stay calm when I am resolving the conflict (handle my emotions).

Never   Always

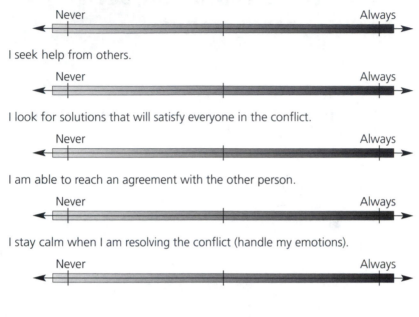

Further reading

Allard, A. and Wilson, J. (1995) *Gender Dimensions: Developing Interpersonal Skills in the Classroom*, Eleanor Curtain Publishing, South Yarra.

AusAID in Reid-Nguyen, R. (ed.) (1999) *Think Global: Global Perspectives for the Lower Primary Classroom*, Curriculum Corporation, Carlton South.

Bessell, H. and Palomares, U. (1973) *Methods in Human Development*, La Mesa Human Development Training Institute, California.

Condliffe, P. (1991) *Conflict Management: A Practical Guide*, TAFE Publications, Vic.

Fuller, A., Bellhouse, B. and Johnson, G. (2001) *The Heart Masters*, Ridgway, Vic.

Graves, N. and Graves, T. (1990) *A Part to Play: Tips, Techniques & Tools for Learning Cooperatively*, Latitude Publications, Vic.

Hancock, K. and Blaby, B. (1989) *People Interacting: Self-awareness, Communication, Social Skills & Problem Solving*, Nelson, Melbourne.

Johnson, W. and Johnson, T. (1987) *Creative Conflict*, Interaction Book Co, Minnesota.

McGrath, H. and Francey, S. (1991) *Friendly Kids, Friendly Classrooms*, Longman, South Melbourne.

McGrath, H. (1997) *Dirty Tricks: Classroom Games for Teaching Social Skills*, Longman, South Melbourne.